# Ethos
# Challenges
# of Right
# and Wrong

## Herman Statum

Professional Press
Chapel Hill, NC 27515-4371

Manufactured in the United States of America
15  16  17  18  19                    10 9 8 7 6 5 4 3 2 1

# Table of Contents

# Foreword

I have learned along the journey of life that individuals cross my path for a reason, season, or lifetime. I have worked alongside many professionals that are to be commended for their outstanding accomplishments. I admire these individuals and I can honestly state that I have learned myriad of professional and personable skills from colleagues that through their examples, have aided me in my years of teaching; sharing their expertise and knowledge, as well as much wisdom. It is without a doubt that the author of this book, Mr. Herman Statum is within the top five most astonishing and extraordinary intellects I have ever had the pleasure of working with.

When Mr. Statum asked me to write a foreword for his book, I found myself both humbled and grateful that a man of countless achievements would allow me the privilege of writing my thoughts for his published works. The following pages you are about to embark on is a compilation of memorable learning moments that were experienced by this incredibly well-versed author. Mr. Statum analyzes the significance of ethical behavior. Mr. Statum is not only a fellow believer of our creator, but he is a man of integrity and highly respected by many in his profession. In his short stories, you will find yourself both enlightened and in wonderment as he describes the importance of good ethics and making decisions to do what is right, even when no one is looking. He holds high standards in his own life and scrutinizes the foundation of his ethical behavior in an array of contexts.

I am certain that anyone that reads this book will find it to be an excellent read as well as a reminder of how our society as a whole has lost the art of good ethical behavior. Whether your beliefs be Biblically-based, knowing we reap what we sow, or if you rely on Karma and feel that what goes around comes around, is irrelevant, because the pages to follow will provide good examples of the Golden Rule and the role it has played throughout his intellectual and spiritual journey in life.

I recommend this book wholeheartedly to all audiences due to the nature of the simple, yet intellectual design. It will leave you with a warm fuzzy feeling and provide as a guide throughout your life. It reminds me of the kind of advice a grandfather would leave behind for his loved ones. The irony is that this book is actually dedicated to his grandchildren and his parents. If you have ever questioned yourself about the choices you make, read this book and you will understand the impact that the general theme plays in our lives and our society. I completely concur with Mr. Statum as he has stated, "It is never wrong to do right and it is never right to do wrong." My prayer is that every individual that reads this book will feel the way I did after reading it and the words between the pages will etch on their hearts a feeling of gratitude; gratitude for the gentle reminders this book portrays and that being kinder than necessary really is a simple matter that goes a long way.

Enjoy your journey through this book!

*Dr. Evelyn Gail Apgar*

# Introduction

As an individual I entered this world alone, and all alone, shall I depart from it. All of us here now share the same earthly destiny—we will some day depart. So the time we are here, we are on a journey starting at birth and ending at death. On the journey we are not alone because billions of other people are here too. How we interact with others has a major impact on all aspects of our being. Our being is essentially our character or the real person we are.

For years, I have been a student of ethics. The more I learned about ethics, the more I wanted to know. I respect and enjoy the subject. I am fascinated by its purity and simple lessons for increasing human effectiveness. Some people have achieved success and financial wealth, but still feel like an underachiever because their strength of character is weak.

I have enjoyed teaching ethics in college courses and giving presentations on ethics to various professional groups and organizations. During my lectures and presentations, I always start with the definition of ethics as simply coming from the Greek word "ethos" which means character. Perhaps the best definition of character is simply what we do or how we act when no one is watching. In his famous I have a dream speech, Doctor Martin Luther

King advised us to judge people by the "content of their character."

The theme of this book is that it is never wrong to do right and never right to do wrong.

# Dedication

This is dedicated to my wonderful grandchildren—
Maya, Jonah, Luke and Seth,
and to the memory of my loving parents—
Fred Carney Statum, Sr. and
Annie Laura Cobble Statum.

## Foundations

Thousands died for my freedom—only one died for my soul—our Lord, Jesus Christ.

Even the youngest among us is taught how kindness matters. The essence of this was coined long ago as the Golden Rule. Simply, when we treat other people as we wish to be treated our outlook improves and happiness results.

This is the day the Lord has made; be glad and rejoice in it. Bible scholars know this verse and believers do not challenge its voracity.

The ancient Greek philosopher Plutarch said that character is a long-standing habit. He also said, "It is in the small, apparently trivial act, that character is most accurately reflected."

Ethics—from where did the term come? It comes from the Greek word Ethos, which means character. So we can see, character and ethics involve both action and inaction or the simple failure to do what we should do. This brings out the real heart of the matter, which is, "It is never wrong to do right and never right to do wrong." This is an effective and easily understood truism which should be a guide for everyone.

## Tunkasila (Grandfather) and Takoja (Grandchild) in Sioux Land

In Sioux land of South Dakota, heavy rains caused streams to leave their banks and all rivers were swollen. A young Sioux maiden was walking with her grandfather. As the pair approached a small, narrow log footbridge, the grandfather said, "Maya, take my hand." The wise maiden said, "No Tunkasila, you take my hand because I may get scared and let go. If you take my hand, I know you will never let me fall." In some form or other, many of us likely had someone who would never let us fall. At the time, we often did not realize the support or help we received. Still, it was there.

# Bus From the Pentagon

It was late in the afternoon after a long, busy day at work when I boarded a Metro bus at the Pentagon and headed to my home in Fairfax, Virginia. Luckily, an end seat was open in a forward row near the front of the bus. I was glad and looked forward to some downtime and a bit of leisure on the ride home. But, that was not to be. The line of passengers loading the bus was long and people boarding went to the rear and had to stand holding the handrails. Soon, the bus capacity was reached and one of the last passengers getting aboard was a middle-aged lady who looked tired, but a bit relieved not to have missed the bus. I then knew what must be done. I stood up, smiled, looked directly at the lady and said softly, "Ma'am, please take this seat." She looked pleasantly surprised and said, "Are you sure because you don't have to do this colonel." I said, "Yes ma'am I do and I am not going very far." Somehow the lady seemed not to believe me completely. Well, that may have been stretching the truth, or a "little white lie" about not going far. On the other hand, distances can be relative and it is only 16 miles from the Pentagon to Kings Park West in Fairfax, Virginia where I lived with my wife and daughter.

Here is the dilemma. I knew I would not disembark from the bus until one of its last stops, but I did not want the lady to refuse my offer, or to feel bad for causing someone to stand. Sometimes circumstances can cause us to be less than completely truthful. Here is where we employ ethics and hold supreme the belief that it is never wrong to do right, and never right to do wrong. Another reason I gave up my comfort on that bus was the slogan of the Boy Scouts of America, which is simply, "Do a good turn daily."

When I joined the Boy Scouts as youngster, I recall taking an oath. The Boy Scout Oath or Promise states "On my honor, I will do my best to do my duty to God and my country and to obey the Scout law; To help other people at all times; To keep myself physically strong, mentally awake and morally straight. The Boy Scout Law states a scout is:

Trustworthy,
Loyal,
Helpful,
Friendly,
Courteous,
Kind,
Obedient,
Cheerful,
Thrifty,
Brave,
Clean,
and Reverent.

As the years passed, I aged out of the scouts and ceased being in a scout troop. But never did I retract my oath, and now as a senior citizen, I still think of myself as a senior boy scout. And why not? Scouting is fun and wholesome and a great activity for helping young boys and girls learn valuable lessons of citizenship and character. I sincerely wish that more boys and girls of all national origins, races, creeds and faiths could participate in scouting. It would be good for them and society as a whole.

As the lady was getting off the bus about mid-point of its route, she smiled and said to me, "I kind of doubted that you were not going far." She added, "Still, I thank you very much for being a gentleman and bless you."

As a sidebar to this episode, when I first stood up, a male civilian sitting nearby glared at me disapprovingly. If looks could kill, I would have been slaughtered on the spot. The glaring civilian struck me as a typical bureaucrat who likely didn't like his job. Instead of being upset, I simply felt sorry for the guy.

# Shopping with Kids

Y es, shopping can be fun for some people. For others, especially older males, also known kindly as senior citizens, it brings little joy. It is no mystery that seniors do occasionally forget things, and let's face it; many of us are tight wads who just don't like to spend money. Neither do seniors enjoy standing in lines of any kind, even though we have much more discretionary time than do the "forties" and "fifties" people who are still working.

When a mother goes to the grocery with two or three children, she can have myriad challenges. Some will be obvious while others are not. While walking through the shopping aisles, if an item is knocked off a shelf or falls from a peg hook, does someone reach down to retrieve it and place it back? Unfortunately, it becomes tempting to push it back under a shelf with a foot, or just keep walking. Whatever action is taken, the children will notice and will learn a good lesson or they will witness a bad example. Children are often very observant and they have copycat tendencies. So when mommy, daddy, or even an older sibling does something wrong, the children may follow suit.

# Uncle Nick and Nephews

Good friends are hard to find, difficult to leave, and impossible to forget. One of my best friends and an outstanding military officer, whom I respect highly, is Lieutenant Colonel (retired) Nicholas Chronis. As the name Chronis reveals, Nick's family came from Greece—the land of ethos. Nick is a consummate professional and to me he is Mister Ethos.

Here is an example. One day, Uncle Nick was taking two of his young nephews to an amusement park. The boys were 13 and 14½. As they approached an entrance ticket booth, Nick noticed a sign stating adults $10.00; children 12 and under $6.00. At the booth, Nick said, "Three adult tickets please." The lady in the booth said, "The boys look young so why don't you get one adult and two children's tickets." She added, "No one will know the difference." Nick said, "I cannot do that." The lady repeated that no one would know the difference. Nick looked down at the boys and told the lady that they would know the difference. As Nick and nephews walked away with three adult tickets, the ticket lady waved at Nick and smiled at him approvingly. It is never wrong to do right and never right to do wrong.

I have enjoyed my association with Nick as a friend and also because I always learn something from him.

Speaking of ethics, Nick commented that, "Ethos works universally and it applies just as much to sales clerks, plumbers and food service workers as it does to lawyers, preachers and soldiers."

---

"Try not to become a man of success, rather a man of value."

—Albert Einstein

---

# Tools for Moral Decision Making

An excellent text I have used in college ethics courses is *Reputable Conduct* by Jones and Carlson. These authors write about tools for moral decision making that have been suggested by Michael Josephson, founder and president of the Josephson Institute for Ethics. The tools are the bell, the book, and the candle.

The bell refers to a question people might ask themselves when they are about to make a choice: Are any warning bells going off?" If yes, we should stop and reconsider what we plan to do.

The book refers to laws, regulations, codes or any other form of written guidance. Will my action be lawful and proper, or violate any policy or procedure?

The candle refers simply to how a decision or action might look if it were exposed to the light of day. The lesson here is to ask others for advice or opinions.

"Live as if you were to die tomorrow. Learn as if you were to live forever."

—Mahatma Gandhi

# Clean Hands and Straight Eyes

"Oh Great Spirit whose voice I hear in the wind and whose breath gives life to all the world—hear me, I am small and weak and I need your strength and wisdom. Let me walk in beauty and make my eyes ever behold the red and purple sunset."

The beautiful passage above is the beginning of an "Indian Prayer," copies of which were distributed by the Sioux Indian children of Red Cloud Indian School in Pine Ridge, South Dakota. It is well known that the Indians of North America believe in honor, they value character, and they live ethically.

To continue the prayer—the final two sentences are as follows: "Make me always ready to come to you, with clean hands and straight eyes;" and "So when life fades, as the fading sunset, my spirit may come to you without shame." The purity of this prayer is undeniable. Its message is clear and powerful.

When America was first discovered, the early pioneers encountered the native Americans whom they called Indians. Unfortunately, many of these first encounters were unfriendly and even hostile. There was an immediate language issue and little to no basis for mutual trust. Over time, the situation improved to the point of the first thanksgiving.

Looking to the future, what might be the experience of our grandchildrens' grandchildren when aliens come to our planet or earthlings travel intergalactically? What parent or grandparent today would not like to know the outcome of such futuristic meetings? We won't be there and can only hope that future earthlings will have, by then, outgrown the pettiness, envy, fear, mistrust, and prejudices toward others who are different.

# A Child of the Universe

In the eighth paragraph of his Desiderata, Max Ehrmann referred to us as a child of the universe, no less than the trees and the stars. In his last paragraph, Ehrmann espoused that with all its sham, drudgery and broken dreams, it is still a beautiful world. Who can deny his eloquence or question the wisdom of such a masterpiece created in 1927.

As children of the universe, we humans share our planet with trillions of living creatures. Some are small and some are large. All are important when we note Ehrmann's statement that "whether or not it is clear to you, no doubt the universe is unfolding as it should." Over the centuries, we homosapiens have changed with advances in science and technology all the way from the days of the caveman's torch to the microwave and iPad devices. Lacking science and technology, changes in our animal friends have been less dramatic, but have had more to do with adaptations to the climate changes, evolution and environmental situations.

It may never be known if our animal friends have tried to learn from humans. But, there are lessons we should note from them. The two species we'll look at briefly are the wolf and the eagle. They are very different creatures; one on the ground and one in the air. Wolves are very social creatures. Probably the best description of the wolf's lifestyle is found in "The Wolf Credo." It was developed after years of research, study and observation of the species of canis lupus—the wolf. The credo says: respect the elders; teach the young; cooperate with the pack; play when you can; hunt when you must; rest in between; share your affections; voice your feelings; and leave your mark. These nine simple behaviors regulate the actions of individual wolves and ensure the balance within the wolf pack. No doubt that we humans would live better if we had such a credo and followed it.

The second animal is the eagle. Very different from he wolf, the eagle is a winged creature, which spends much time in the air. Compared to other winged creatures, such as turkeys in flocks or quail in coveys, the eagle often flies alone. Over the years, humans have respected the eagle's majestic appearance and prowess. Our Native Americans placed the highest value on feathers of the eagle. Throughout the United States, eagles are protected by game laws. The eagle's glory and place in history was secured with the selection of the bald eagle as the official symbol of the United States. The highest rank in Boy Scouts is the Eagle Award. Less known is the fact that the highest rank in the Girl Scouts is the Gold Award. Not to criticize the choices of parents or drivers, but it is hard not to notice a disparity between the numbers of bumper stickers of Eagle Scouts over Gold Awards. The "My Son is an Eagle Scout" sticker is seen far more often than stickers for the Gold Award.

Similar to a lesson from the wolf, we humans can also learn from the eagle family. Mother eagle knows instinctively when young eagles should leave the nest. Since their hatching, the eaglets have been fed and cared for by their parents. At a certain point, mother eagle will physically remove them from the nest. She knows that unless the young ones begin to use those great wings, they will not be able to feed themselves. Also, the nest has only so much room and eagles grow to large sizes. Now, let us apply these factors to the human family. How long do parents allow Johnny to stay home beyond the teenage years? If he or she is not in college or attending technical training, should he continue to sleep until mid-morning, watch TV, and play video games for hours, then enjoy a nice dinner after the parents come home from work? If the child is always given everything, instead of working and earning a living, it will fail to develop a healthy level of confidence and self-respect. In my ethics course, I often use portions of a speech Bill Gates gave at a high school about 11 things students did not and will not learn in school. Bill's rule one is: "Life is not fair—get used to it." His rule two is: "The world won't care about your self-esteem. The world will expect you to accomplish something before you feel good about yourself."

A new grandmother gave me a copy of a paper she had received from her mother years ago. It is precious and here it is. "Some day when my children are old enough to understand the logic that motivates a mother, I will tell them:

- I loved you enough to ask where you were going, with whom, and what time you would be home.

- I loved you enough to insist that you save your money to buy a bike for yourself even though we could afford to buy one for you.

- I loved you enough to be silent and let you discover your new best friend was a creep.

- I loved you enough to make you take a Milky Way back to the drugstore (with a bite out of it) and tell the clerk, "I stole this yesterday and want to pay for it."

- I loved you enough to stand over you for two hours while you cleaned your room, a job that would have taken me 15 minutes.

- I loved you enough to let you see anger, disappointment and tears in my eyes. Children must learn that their parents are not perfect.

- I loved you enough to let you assume the responsibility for your actions even when the penalties were so harsh they almost broke my heart.

But most of all, I loved you enough to say no when I knew you would hate me for it. Those were the most difficult battles of all. I'm glad I won them, because in the end you won something, too." —Author Unknown

"Look deep into nature, and you will understand everything better."

—Albert Einstein

# The 10-10-80 Rule in Security

With over 30 years experience in security, assets protection, loss prevention, and emergency planning, I have seen progress in technology of access control, closed-circuit television, and alarm systems. Growth continues in these areas with multi-billion dollar markets. It is also clear that a good protective services program will contain a blend of people, equipment and procedures. In security, we try to deny access to unauthorized individuals and to detect and deter theft and wrongdoing.

In most situations, and especially in retail, the hazards of shoplifting and external theft are ever present. But, the biggest loss often comes from within. Some managers call it internal theft and others term it as employee dishonesty. Experience shows that the most effective tool against employee dishonesty still remains that of effective pre-employment screening. In other words, be very selective in the hiring process and do not employ ethically-challenged people.

In the selection and hiring process, good managers are aware of a rule that has been around for a long time. It is the 10-10-80 rule that appears simple, but is very accurate. Essentially, 10% of the people you hire will not lie, cheat or steal because they cannot. These individuals have strong convictions, self-respect, and willpower to always do what is right. They also are controlled by a conscience that will not compromise with mediocrity in honor. Completely opposite are the second 10% who essentially will lie, cheat or steal with little or no hesitation. They are narcissistic and delight in getting something for nothing. The best, and often the only, protection against this 10% is to avoid hiring them in the first place.

The big 80% of employees will essentially remain honest and ethical if the company or business has clear rules, meaningful controls and appropriate supervision. The goal of leaders and management is to help these people to stay honest. If employees feel that management values commitment, loyalty and honesty they are less tempted to violate controls. Employees also perform better and work harmoniously when they experience the emotional security of a disciplined environment.

# Why Some People Do Wrong: Lie, Cheat, Steal, Fraud, Violate Rules

When asked to write a list of why some people do wrong, my college ethics class of criminal justice students identified these:

- Financial gain. What employees would not want to increase their "take home money" even without a raise in pay?

- Indebtedness. Living beyond means.

- Medical bills.

- Gambling debts.

- Alcohol and drug abuse, including abuse of prescription medications.

- Little fear of being caught.

- Weak controls by company.

- Poor leadership by management or supervisors.

- To get even with the company for some perceived wrong or injustice.

The reasons above are some of the most common situations of wrongdoing. During some of my investigations where the evidence was conclusive in proving guilt, or the suspect admitted stealing, some people actually blamed the company. Excuses such as "the company was too lax in its controls making it too easy to take cash or write up phony refunds." Other wrongdoers have explained it this way: "The company is to blame for the mess I am in now because if it had caught my first few thefts I would have stopped and not got in deeper and deeper." As he was being terminated for serious rule violations, a store manager commented arrogantly that he had driven through stop signs on his street everyday and would keep doing it because he has yet to receive a ticket. With such flawed logic, this poor fellow is a danger to other people and to himself. He failed to understand that the purpose of traffic signs is to control traffic for safety and not just to give police a reason to write tickets.

President Ronald Reagan gave us some sound advice when he advised that, "We must reject the idea that every time a law is broken, society is guilty rather than the law-breaker. It is time to restore the American precept that the individual is accountable for his/her actions."

# Codes of Conduct

Over the years, the military has faced various ethical challenges causing great concern at all levels. The military code of conduct addresses those situations and decision areas that all military members could encounter to some degree. It is a six-article code that provides general guidelines for the daily conduct of all military personnel. It includes basic information useful to U.S. prisoners of war in efforts to exploit them to the advantage of the enemy's cause and their own disadvantage.

Additional to its combat capabilities and impressive array of lethal weapons, the U.S. military could always be proud of its service academies. The United States Military Academy at West Point, New York; the United States Naval Academy at Annapolis, Maryland; and the United States Air Force Academy at Colorado Springs, Colorado continue to produce commissioned officers for the military. Many of the nation's top officers graduated from an academy. Included are names like Eisenhower, MacArthur, and Haig. Another of the nation's most brilliant leaders did not attend a service academy, but received his military commission through the Reserve Officers Training Corps (ROTC) program. At one of his speeches at a large convention, General Colin Powell remarked that when he joined

the Army his goal was to retire as an 0-5, lieutenant colonel, but he didn't. Instead he left the U.S. Army at its
highest rank, an 0-10, four-star general. He also served
at the military's highest level as Chairman of the Joint
Chiefs of Staff. Colin Powell later served the nation as the
United States Secretary of State. All of this is an impressive resume for a guy born of Jamaican immigrants, growing up in New York, with a goal of retiring as a lieutenant
colonel.

Back in the sixties and seventies, the military estab-
lishment went through some challenging times. The Vietnam War occupied the news for several years. For those
of us who were honored to serve there and lucky enough
to come home, it gave us a special perspective on life that
we otherwise may not have today. To appreciate the meaning of life, you must have been faced with the danger of
losing it—and that is a feeling the protected shall never
know. In 1971 during my second tour in Vietnam, the late
Marvin Gaye's song "What's Going On" was released and
it remains as one of my favorites. Referring to the war,
Marvin (1939-1984) sang "Mother, mother there are too
many of you crying," and "Brother, brother there are far
too many of you dying." This song expressed some of the
realities of war and it touched me emotionally.

Like all wars, the best in people can come out, and
the worst can happen. The latter happened at the My Lai
massacre during which an entire Vietnamese village was
burned and many of its inhabitants, including women and
children, were killed by U.S. soldiers. The only foot soldier
who refused to participate in the massacre was Michael

Bernhardt. Another hero at the My Lai incident was U.S. Army Captain Hugh Thompson, a helicopter pilot. He landed his helicopter between the soldiers and the villagers and ordered the soldiers to stop shooting. Over a loudspeaker, Captain Thompson announced that if they did not stop shooting he would have his door gunner to fire on them. It worked and many innocent lives were saved. That day, the innocence of many young U.S. soldiers was also spared when they came to realize that shooting of unarmed, innocent women and children is never justified, not even in the heat of battle. Initially, Bernhardt and Thompson were criticized, but later both were hailed for their courage.

The U.S. military academies do their best to provide excellent academic programs. They also instill values in the cadets with slogans like duty, honor and country. Because of their overall high standards for selection and admittance, the academies normally experience fewer incidents of misconduct and ethical violations. But, they do occur and are of particular embarrassment to the Department of Defense. Cheating and harassment remain as two of the main violations. Each of the academies has tried to raise the level of awareness about moral values and ethics. They have implemented their individual codes of conduct. The U.S. Naval Academy's code of conduct says, "We will not lie, cheat or steal, nor tolerate those who do."

Particularly troubling to the military has been the misconduct of senior leaders. Of the 18 generals and admirals fired in recent years, 10 lost their jobs because of sex-related offenses. Not included in the tally was a retired Army, four-star general who was forced to resign as director of a large federal agency after an affair with a woman who was writing the biography of his military career. Topping all incidents were allegations against a former commander-in-chief accused of inappropriate contact in the White House with a female intern.

An element of society that is held to a high standard is law enforcement. We all expect the police to uphold their mission, which is to protect and to serve. School teachers and police officers are still two of society's best bargains. The actions of both are expected to meet high standards. Law enforcement has an Oath of Honor. It says, "On my honor, I will never betray my badge, my integrity, my character, or the public trust. I will always have the courage to hold myself and others accountable for their actions. I will always uphold the Constitution, my community and the agency I serve." Wouldn't it be helpful if politicians at all levels had a similar standard and followed it?

# Our Teachers and Mentors

I t is true that in the end, most of us will have more regrets over the things that we did not do than regrets over the things we did. As the saying goes, "Hindsight is 20/20." Along life's journey we sometimes seek shortcuts or bypasses. Unfortunately, we can find crutches to ease burdens and let creature comfort lead us into mediocracy. A lesson many people overlooked in their career planning was that instead of aiming too high in their goals and missing, they aimed too low and hit.

On the positive side, our better coaches in sports tell us that, "When the going gets tough—the tough get going." Another term we hear is simply, "No pain, no gain," especially in rowing competitions. "That which I endure shall make me stronger" can be a good elixir also in some situations. From our first auto maker, Henry Ford, we heard, "Whether you think you can or think you cannot, you are probably right." Our grandparents were the ones who reminded us of the fact that, "Only you alone can make yourself be a failure." This brings up the point of what is success and what is failure. One of my favorite psychologists and experts in human motivation, Abraham Maslow (1908-1970), created the widely-acclaimed Hierarchy of Needs. In the form of a pyramid, the physiological needs were at the base. Going up the pyramid are safety, love/belonging, esteem, and up to the summit is self-actualization. This top level occurs when people reach a state of harmony and understanding because they are engaged in their full potential. My first encounter with Maslow's Hierarchy of Needs was during the research phase of writing my masters degree thesis for the University of Southern California.

Looking back all the way from elementary school, high school, college, and through graduate school, I have been blessed with excellent teachers. Each teacher did his or her best, and I am thankful for their professionalism and superb guidance. Not only did they educate me in the required subjects and basic curriculum, they taught me about life and motivated me to be all that I could be.

In front of the desk in my den is my favorite antique chair. In addition to its value as an antique, the chair is more special because it belonged to my favorite high school teacher, Mrs. Ruby Wallace. Mrs. Wallace was an outstanding educator and a wonderful person who was respected and admired by everyone who knew her. My family and I were living in Virginia at the time of her passing and had not known of her illness. I bought the chair later at the auction of her estate. Many times I have regretted not visiting Mrs. Wallace after I became a teacher and telling her of my admiration, respect and appreciation. God bless you, Mrs. Wallace.

From my mother, I learned the value of effort, sacrifice, commitment and hard work. She always put her four sons first and we knew it. Mother loved nature and her Lord and she followed the golden rule in all her daily activities. A lesson from my mother was that blue ribbons, trophies and first-place finishes are fine. But, more important is how we feel, win or lose, at the finish. If we did not get first place, but did our best, we did not lose or fail because the only real failure in life is the failure to try. Mother taught me that only I can make myself a failure and people who blame others are using emotional crutches. Many coaches of sports teams have been wise enough to know that even when their team won a particular game it was not because the players did well, but they prevailed mainly because their opponent lacked energy in the last quarter or made too many errors. Winning coaches spot weaknesses in their game plans and their players and get busy fixing what needs fixing. These coaches also understand the wisdom of the legendary mentor, Coach Vince Lombardi, for whom the Super Bowl trophy is named. Lombardi was a perfectionist who made his players understand that practice does not make perfect, rather "Perfect practice makes perfect." Having a wonderful daughter who is a Special Olympian, my wife and I learned to appreciate things more fully. To observe how these athletes enjoy just competing is heart warming. They don't have to win every time to be happy because the Special Olympics Oath says, "Let me win, but if I cannot win, let me be brave in the attempt."

My father taught all of us about manners and doing the right thing. One of his main teachings was to judge other people objectively and fairly. He explained why or how we should not judge people by what others may say about them, but rather judge them by the way treat us.

Looking for work as a young man during the Great Depression, my father gladly took a job as an ice man in a large city. This was before the popular electric refrigerators, or "frigidaires," as they were sometimes called. The icemen literally carried large blocks of ice to and inside buildings, houses and apartments. When my father was assigned to his ice route, some of the other icemen teased him because his route went into an area known to house organized crime families and gangsters. My father was always punctual and friendly and he was rewarded well. He tells accounts of seeing guys with broad white ties in a room smoking fine Havana cigars with large Thompson submachine guns on a table. What he did not hear was loud swearing or anger. It was a business- like atmosphere and my father who was earning about thirty cents an hour, was treated courteously and with respect. He always received substantial tips, which he appreciated. To keep the other ice men from being envious, my father let them believe what they had assumed and he did not bother to tell them just how "tough" his gangster customers really were not.

Growing up in Tennessee where the winters can get fairly cold, I cannot ever recall seeing my father wearing a jacket. I am not sure he even owned a coat of any kind. On the coldest days, he would wear a heavy flannel shirt and sometimes a sweater, but not a coat. He also never got the flu or a cold. Being an ice man had some side advantages and my father believed that colds were caused by germs and not by the temperature. That makes sense doesn't it? Looking back at my father being an ice man, I can draw a similar parallel with my being a soldier in that you can take the boy out of the Army, but you cannot take the Army out of the boy. Neither can you melt the spirit of a true ice man.

# I Shall Pass This Way But Once

"Any good, therefore, that I can do, or any kindness that I can show, let me do it now. Let me not deter or neglect it for I shall not pass this way again"

—Author Unknown

Too often we are remiss in not doing something good to aid or help another by thinking we will do it later. The danger of such procrastination is that the opportunity for such may never recur and will be lost forever. How often have we failed to hug a parent or told them we loved them, only to see them later in a lifeless state, or they were overcome with Alzheimer's or dementia?

When we think of an old buddy or a friend we've not seen in a long time, the idea flashes to us that maybe we should go see them soon. The term "soon" can be elusive as to some people it is next month, while to others it may mean next year. Either way, we have to understand that tide and time wait for no person.

After losing two good friends last year, and remembering the movie The Bucket List, I decided to make a list. First on the list was to visit old friends and Army buddies that I had not seen in 30 years in the Virginia-Washington D.C. area. I made the trip, and I'm glad that I did. It is clear that for several friends visited, I have now seen them for the last time. During the trip, I visited, for the first time, the gravesite of my wedding's best man in Arlington National Cemetery. It was a very moving experience that I shall never forget. With age, many people come to realize that great friends are hard to find, difficult to leave and impossible to forget.

# Angels Among Us

From early civilizations to the present, people have wondered about angels. Do they exist? Where are they? What do they look like? Can we talk to them? These questions may remain unanswered for centuries to come, if ever at all. For scientists, facts proving angels do not exist. For believers, hard evidence is not needed. The depictions or images that have appeared in pictures show human-like beings with wings. Sometimes when a person is spared serious injury in a horrific vehicle accident, or pulled safely from a burning building, the onlookers will make comments like "that person surely had a guardian angel." The bottom line is that angels, real or imagined, are good. They appear to use super natural powers with splendor, grace and compassion.

In the global community, if those people who believe in angels are asked to identify such angels, Mother Teresa would be a big winner.

"She was one of the great spiritual servants of our era, whose simple wisdom expressed untold depths of devotion."

—President Jimmy Carter

The blessed Teresa of Calcutta (August 26, 1910-September 5, 1997) was an Albanian-born Indian Roman Catholic Religious Sister who belonged to the world and made it a better place.

Many ordinary people have experienced events that are extraordinary and surpass logical explanations. One such event happened a few years ago with my wife and youngest daughter. Soon after losing my job, they drove to Georgia to visit our oldest daughter who was working there. Driving back home to Tennessee, my wife and daughter were behind a few cars following a large truck on the interstate highway. Suddenly, without warning, a large metal block, used to keep the vehicle from rolling when parked, fell from underneath the truck onto the roadway. Some cars, including my wife's, hit the block, which blew out a front tire. Unable to avoid collisions, some cars struck other cars and the interstate was cluttered with damaged vehicles. The state police, local law enforcement and medical units responded well. The response by the trucking company was also excellent. They put the spare tire on my wife's car and hosted her and my daughter, along with other accident victims, for a night's stay in a motel just off the interstate. As my wife was driving by a service station en route to the motel, she and my daughter saw a woman sitting in a car with three young children. The woman was crying. My wife approached the woman and asked had her family been involved in the accident on the highway. The woman replied that they were not involved and did not know of the accident.

Still curious about what was wrong, my wife asked could she help. The woman explained that they needed a tire for the car to get back to Indiana. Her husband was out looking for a tire, but they had very little money. In the spirit of a Bavarian girl, and a good Samaritan, my wife went into action. She asked the attendant at the service station if she could cash a check for money to help the family. The attendant said that she could not accept an out-of-state personal check. She apologized, but asked if my wife had a credit card. Then, she advised my wife how to get money from the station's ATM using her credit card. It worked out and my wife gave the family $100.00 in cash. The next morning as my wife and daughter were starting to leave, they stopped at the service station to check on the family who had left in the evening. The woman who had been crying asked the station attendant to again thank "That lady from Bavaria" who spoke with an accent because she is an angel for helping strangers on the road to get back home.

After my wife and daughter were back home, I checked their car. The left front tire had completely blown out. But, their car had miraculously not hit another vehicle or struck a retaining wall or other object. Having worked several years in a service station, and later in a tire shop to pay for college, I knew well what often happens when a front tire blows out in such a manner. But they were unharmed and thankfully there were no injuries to occupants of the several vehicles involved in the accident. Was all this just a coincidence with a lot of lucky people on the highway and the family needing help who got it from a stranger? I do not know for sure, but neither can the intervention by a higher power be ruled out simply because it is not yet proven scientifically.

Hebrews 13:2 tells us, "Do not neglect to show hospitality to strangers. For by this some have entertained Angels without knowing it."

# Precious Words and Good Deeds

I n his book, *The Four Agreements*, Miguel Ruiz advises us to "be impeccable" with our words. He explains that we should speak with integrity and say only what we mean. We should avoid using the word to speak against ourselves or to gossip about others. He also advises to use the power of your word in the direction of truth and love.

As children, many of us learned the saying that "sticks and stones may hurt my bones, but words never harm me." This seemed to make sense when we were young; but as we aged, we learned by experience just how harmful words can be. Mean words can be hurtful and make others feel bad. Done in a more malicious or destructive way, especially when intended to damage a person's character or reputation, an individual can be charged with slander. If the words are in writing, the charge becomes libel. Both slander and libel can have legal consequences with sanctions and penalties if substantiated. Ethical conduct and doing the right things will steer us clear of these and other maladies.

There are two precious words that we learn early in life and never outgrow. They are please and thank you. We use please when we want something and thank you when it is received or given. Actually, please is appropriate whether we are the recipient or the giver. Many benevolent philanthropists openly indicate that two main reasons for their generosity are that giving is just the right thing to do and giving makes them feel better. Indeed, it may be hard, if not impossible, to find someone who gives to charity or to a needy person and does not feel good about it. Being honest with ourselves, some of us also get a good feeling about charitable giving because it can be tax deductible.

There is usually little debate over the belief that good people do good things and bad people do bad things. Who are the good people? For our purposes, let's just say they are ethical people of good character who avoid doing bad things most of the time. These good people do not lie, cheat, or steal and comply with the laws and rules of decency. Conversely, we tend to criticize or condemn those people who deviate from good behavior. Can we then generalize by saying that bad people do only bad things? Not really, because a notorious gangster is capable of good deeds. A case in point is Alphonse Capone whose business was crime. One of Capone's sayings was, "You can get more with a kind word and a gun than with a kind word alone." On the other hand, little is known about Capone's benevolence. But the fact is that he financed a large public soup kitchen in New York City during the Great Depression and tried to remain anonymous. This is not the sort of thing bad people do.

"What you are will show in what you do"
—Thomas A. Edison

"I've learned that people will forget what you said, people will forget what you did, but people will never forget how you made them feel."
—Maya Angelou

# The Moral Compass

L ife is regulated by customs, laws, rules and boundaries. Growing up, children learn that obeying parents is generally a good idea. That way, mommy and daddy are pleased which can result in more privileges and treats such as candy, cookies and ice cream. Children also learn, sometimes the hard way, that doing what they shouldn't can have consequences or punishments. These can range from an angry look, a frown, a harsh scolding, being placed in "time out," up to a physical spanking. Growing up as one of four boys, when Mother spanked one of us, she would say, "This is going to hurt me more than you, son." We boys knew that if we yelled like it really hurt, Mother would swing more lightly. Mother used a small branch from one of our peach trees in the back yard. Daddy simply used his leather belt for spankings. And, unlike with Mother, we boys did not yell in pain during Daddy's spankings because he might swing harder.

Looking back, I know that we boys had wonderful parents who always did their best for their children. They were also wonderful grandparents. One of the most tender moments with my parents occurred one evening when I was at home on leave from the Army. I had commented on how they could be proud to have four sons and all graduated from the same college. At that point, Mother started to cry. Then, for the first time, I learned that there had been five of us boys. The baby before me had died at birth. This is a terrible burden for parents to bear. I never knew the baby just before me, but I now think of him as my guardian angel.

In operating a vehicle, our driving is regulated by signage, roadway markings and traffic devices. For the sake of safety, we know that we should wear seat belts, drive defensively and obey traffic rules. Failure to do so can have consequences ranging from dents on the vehicle, to major damages, up to serious injuries and even fatalities. The things just mentioned help control our behavior on the road. But what controls or regulates our behavior, especially toward other people, in the larger areas of life. The answer is our ethos or our character. It is who we really are.

Our thoughts, beliefs and inner feelings form the foundations of our character. Our ethos consists of a lifetime of learning, environmental influences, our culture and the human values we were taught and those we adopted for ourselves. The values we hold uppermost exert great influence on our perceptions and our behaviors. More than just products of our physical environments, we are the products of our values and our thoughts.

Some people will always do right because that is just who they are. Their moral compass is piloted accurately by their conscience. Unfortunately, other people roam on the fringes of morality and they modify their behaviors to fit the controls they perceive to be in effect. In the corporate business world, these people overlook the truth and "tell the boss (chairman, CEO or president) what they want to hear." After all, what executive or leader does not want to hear good news? They also react approvingly and generously toward the messengers of good news. There is nothing wrong with reporting good news. But the good leader wants all the news of significance. The most important aspects of the news must be validity and truthfulness. Initially, large corporations including Enron, WorldCom and Tyco, appeared to do well thriving on good news. Unfortunately, the truth became a victim and these giants stumbled. According to George Orwell, "The further a society drifts from the truth, the more it will hate those who speak it."

Similarly, German theologian Dietrich Bonhoeffer stated, "Silence in the face of evil is itself evil." Three words often heard regarding the cultures in troubled corporations were arrogance, greed and corruption. Their moral compasses failed.

On a larger scale, is the issue of the moral compass for a country? What is our future as a nation seems to be of concern now more than ever. To many people, the moral compass for the United States is not as clear as they would like. To remain optimistic, I recall the wisdom of one of my friends in Bavaria who advised me to remember that a country really consists of only two main elements. They are the land and the people, not a government, which is always temporary. He added that America is a beautiful land and its people are ethical. We also should remember that we did not inherit this land from our forefathers, but we are simply borrowing its use from our grandchildren.

Our challenge is to preserve the beauty of this land and to protect the liberty and freedom we cherish.

# Why People Don't Report
# Wrongdoing

When we were kids, a tag we sought to avoid was "tattle tale'. It was never favorable and caused hurt feelings. We just learned not to tell on a friend, but felt little guilt or remorse when telling on an adversary or someone we did not like. In the adult world, a similar term is "whistleblower" which usually refers to someone who reports wrongdoing. The act can be in the form of cheating, theft, fraud, misappropriation, or embezzlement. The United States Department of Justice and its FBI defines fraud as intentional deception or trickery. From this, the key word is intentional, meaning that to be a crime the act must have been done on purpose, versus simply as a mistake or accident. To embezzle is to appropriate fraudulently to one's own use that which is entrusted to one's care, or that over which the wrongdoer has some degree of control. An example would be a book-keeper who records the accounts of business and who diverts company money or assets to their own use. Since these type crimes are done by stealth in a covert manner, and do not involve violence, they invoke little if any fear, unlike violent crimes such as aggravated assault, rape, robbery and murder. In the area of organized crime such as the Mafia, the term "rat" comes up, especially when criminals report things to the police or pass information to correctional officers or wardens. These are serious situations that have resulted in physical beatings, torture and murder.

In the business world, sometimes theft, fraud and policy violations are not reported because a person witnessing the wrongdoing may only be aware of the symptoms and not be sure it is fraud or a crime. Many people are cautious and simply do not want to wrongly accuse someone. Sometimes, employees don't know whom to tell when they witness criminal behavior or misconduct so they remain silent. Unfortunately, some companies and organizations do not make reporting procedures clear or simple. Other companies, and even the state and federal governments, now encourage whistleblowing through fraud hot lines. Callers can remain anonymous and substantial monetary rewards have been paid in some cases.

When employees observe or witness wrongdoing, especially thefts or crimes, it can be very stressful. It is just human nature to try to avoid involvement in serious situations that do not affect or involve us directly. Anytime we report a situation that may get someone punished, a risk of reprisal becomes possible. Over time, a lesson learned by many employees is also that company leaders and executives like to hear good news. The reverse can also happen, giving rise to the old request, "Please don't shoot the messenger" who may be bringing bad news. In ancient Rome, messengers who gave Caesar bad news were sometimes beheaded.

Below is an example of a case that illustrates some of the dynamics of the reporting of an incident. Names have been changed to protect the innocent. I used the case in one of my college criminal justice courses and the students commented favorably on its value as a tool of learning. The first part is a narrative of the situation where students acted as a Security Director and the second part is a letter to the person who reported the incident initially.

## Incident At Blankville Retail Store

You (students) are the Security Director at the ABC Retail Corporation. Your department secretary received a disturbing telephone call this morning from a cashier at the Blankville Store.

The female caller was nervous and spoke in a low tone that was difficult to understand. At first, the caller was reluctant to give her name. But your secretary consoled her and she gave her name as Trellis Mae Tipster, the head cashier. Trellis alleged that there was dishonesty and misconduct at the Blankville Store. According to Trellis, a retail associate was giving unauthorized discounts to his friends and worse, phony refunds were being made by the store manager. The store manager, who is married, was also harassing an attractive young female part-time associate by asking her to meet him at a motel after work. The victim had confided to Trellis tearfully and was afraid of losing her job. Students, how will you handle the situation? (Going on vacation is not an option if you want to keep your high salary, company car and nice annual bonus.)

In the actual case, the security director met with the company president and outlined his plan for an onsite investigation. The investigation went very smoothly. The store manager, and the associate who had given discounts, were terminated without complications. The young female, who had been harassed by the manager, was promoted to full time status. She became a star employee with a great attitude and appeared to be on track to becoming a manager trainee and likely the manager of her own store later. The case illustrates the values of loyalty. Trellis was loyal to the corporation and the corporation wisely responded appropriately and effectively to Trellis as noted in a personal letter to her from a high ranking official within one day of her initial call.

Here is a version of the letter to Trellis sent to her home address.

Dear Trellis:

This is to let you know that we appreciate the information you provided us recently.

We are very sorry that the problems you reported have occurred in the Blankville Store. The ABC Corporation tries hard to keep the conditions in all stores as pleasant and as professional as possible, and it is disappointing when things go wrong. But, you can be assured we will follow up on the matters you reported and appropriate actions will be taken as may be warranted by our investigation this week.

Your information will be kept confidential. Please also be assured that no criticism or adverse action is ever permitted against persons who provide such information.

Thanks again for your loyalty and your special contribution to ABC Corporation.

Sincerely,

Melvin Strong
Executive Vice President

# Studies on Ethics

There is universal agreement that there is a positive correlation between a company's reputation and its market share. Studies in all fields also show that views are mixed on integrity and ethics in the workplace. Here are some of the more common views in business overall.

- Less than half (47%) of employees believe their senior leaders are people of high integrity.

- A slight majority (56 %) of employees feel that integrity has been well-communicated internally.

- Only a third (34%) of employees feel comfortable reporting misconduct.

- Some of the findings of studies of ethics in government include the following.

- Public administration employees, including federal, state and local government workers, are among the most negative about ethics in the workplace.

- Over 21% of government workers could not agree with the statement, "Overall, my organization is highly ethical," contrasted to only 5% in the financial services industry.

- More than one in four workers (27%) doubt that their senior leaders "Are people of high integrity."

- Only 27% in the government were comfortable reporting misconduct, compared to 40% in healthcare and 41% in retail. However, in recent years government has improved in encouraging its workers to come forward in reporting misconduct, fraud, waste and abuse.

A useful outcome of various studies has been to show companies and professional organizations the need and value of a code of ethics. An organization of licensed professional investigators to which I belong in my state realized that it needed a code of ethics. I volunteered to write it and here is an approved version.

## Association of Licensed Professional Investigators (ALPI)

## Code of Ethics

## Preamble

The ALPI, hereinafter referred to as the Association, recognizes the vital importance of the willingness of its members to always act with honesty and integrity. Members will operate within the letter and spirit of applicable laws and decency. Members will bring appropriate skills and capability to every client assignment and will remain objective in forming professional opinions, findings and the advice they render. Members will remain committed to fair business practices and will ensure they receive appropriate fees that accurately reflect the value of the services provided. Guided by the basic truth that it is never right to do wrong and never wrong to do right, the Association adopts the following code and mandates its strict observance as a binding condition to membership in or affiliation with ALPI.

## Code of Ethics

I. A member shall perform professional services in accordance with the law and highest moral principles.

II. A member shall not engage in any illegal activity or unethical conduct or any activity which would constitute a conflict of interest.

III. A member shall exhibit the highest level of integrity in the performance of all assignments and will accept only assignments for which there is a reasonable expectation that the assignment will be completed with professional competence.

IV. A member shall comply with lawful orders of the courts and will testify, when required, to matters truthfully and without bias or prejudice.

V. A member shall reveal all matters discovered during the course of the investigation, which if omitted, would cause a distortion of the facts.

VI. A member shall not maliciously injure the reputation of competitors, colleagues, clients or customers.

VII. A member shall safeguard confidential or sensitive information and will exercise due care to prevent improper disclosure or misuse of the information.

Any member who knows, or has reasonable grounds to believe, that another member has failed to conform to the Association's Code of Ethics will report such to the ALPI President.

"Love all, trust a few, do wrong to none."

—William Shakespeare

# Those Less Fortunate

"Let me win, but if I cannot win, let me be brave in the attempt." That is the oath of Special Olympics. Today, Special Olympics is a growing global movement of people who want to improve the lives of people with intellectual disabilities. It all began in the 1950's and early 1960's when Eunice Kennedy Shriver ( JFK's sister) saw how unjustly and unfairly people with intellectual disabilities were treated. She also saw that many children didn't even have a place to play. Eunice decided to take action and she achieved remarkable results as the founder and mother of Special Olympics. Today, Special Olympics' global reach expands to 4.4 million athletes around the world. Census numbers also show that as many as 80,000 events and competitions are held annually.

Eunice Kennedy Shriver was born on July 10, 1921 and she passed on August 11, 2009.

Like Mother Teresa, Eunice was respected and loved for her humanity and her wonderful service to those less fortunate. In paying tribute to Eunice Kennedy Shriver after her death, Nelson Mandela, former president of South Africa, said so eloquently, "Her voice will echo each time the oath is recited, her fire will burn each time the flame is lighted, and her legacy will live and grow through every athlete in every competition, daily, around the world."

In 2001, our youngest daughter participated as an athlete at the Special Olympics World Winter Games in Alaska. She competed in downhill skiing and is forever proud of the Olympic medals she won there. At the opening ceremony evening dinner, my wife was seated at the head table next to Eunice Kennedy Shriver and had the honor of introducing Eunice to the international participants. The World Winter Games was a very memorable event for my wife and daughter. Over the years, Special Olympics has been a blessing and rewarding experience for my family and many other people. For the parents of the Special Olympics athletes and many supporters, the following quote is offered, "What we have done for ourselves, dies with us; what we have done for others and the world remains immortal."

Growing up, my three brothers and I learned some valuable lessons from our parents.

One of the first things they taught us was the golden rule of treating others as we want to be treated. We were taught that the only real failure in life is the failure to try. Our parents also helped us to understand that whatever happens to us in life is not as important as our reaction to it. Adverse events can make people bitter or better. Lou Holtz, former Notre Dame University Football Coach and sports celebrity, stated that, "I am convinced that life is 10 percent of what happens to me and 90% of how I react to it. And so it is with you—we are in charge of our attitudes."

Modern society has done much to help people with disabilities, whether the impairment is physical or mental. Hand rails, wheel chair ramps, special access devices and handicapped parking spots all can help people with special needs. Generally, most people follow the rules and do not abuse special parking arrangements. But unfortunately, some motorists do park where they should not. In their way of thinking, parking improperly in a handicapped-only space is okay if you are running late or pressed for time and no other spaces are available. The last time I drove my daughter to a video rental store we witnessed a violation of handicapped-only parking. We drove into the parking lot and parked in an open, unmarked space several yards from the store's entrance. As we approached the entrance, a late model luxury vehicle pulled in to one of the two open handicapped spaces directly in front of the entrance door. The driver and lone occupant was a woman in a sporty jogging suit in her late forties or early fifties. The woman appeared to take a plastic hang tag from the glove compartment and hang it on the rear view mirror. The tag was a standard blue handicapped parking tag. The woman then walked briskly the short distance into the store. As she opened the door, the woman glanced back at me looking briefly at her tag. My daughter and I finished our business and exited the store about the same time as the woman. As we were walking out, the woman looked a bit annoyed at me and said, "That handicapped tag is for my mother." I replied, "Sorry, I did not see your mother with you." The woman asked me, "Are you a policeman?" I said no ma'am, I am a senior boy scout and I wish you a pleasant evening.

At that point, we just smiled at each other and left. Years ago, a friend and I were talking about handicapped parking spaces and I recall him asking did I ever park in one. I said I never would because I would be afraid of something happening to make me be qualified for handicapped privileges.

# Sweet Bird of Youth

Oh sweet bird of youth, fly not away too soon. While there are those who question the existence of The Almighty, most people do believe in God and in heaven in one form or another. Most people have yet to meet someone who believes in heaven and doesn't want to go there. Sure, we believers want to go to heaven, but just not so soon. It really boils down to a matter of timing.

The last time I was in San Francisco it was to give a presentation at a workshop seminar. Versus staying in my hotel room, reviewing my presentation slides and notes, I decided to see more of that beautiful city. The weather was perfect and I enjoyed the scenery and fresh air. At one of the quaint little shops I entered, there was a small plaque that I shall always remember. It read "Time, that is the stuff life is made of. Always use it wisely and never waste it. Above all, allow no one else to use it for you."

The message of that little plaque is clear and precious. It reminds me of another small plaque that once hung in my mother's kitchen. It reads simply, "Do not resent to grow old—many are denied the privilege." My loving Mother went to see her precious Jesus at the age of 92. Her plaque now hangs on the wall in my den.

es of Right and Wrong

San Francisco was in 1966 dur-
new wife from Tennessee, where
ave, to California where I would
first tour there. My wife would
iting family friends then fly back
er parents during my time away.
ake the trip to California by car
try that she had only read about.
it deepened my appreciation for
and. As one who has done it, I
friends that they should put a
on their bucket lists and do it.
wstone National Park and many
pretty images in videos and pic-
ompare with the natural beauty
here in person. During our drive
nted to see Disneyland and we
a Monday without knowing the
d on Mondays. But the monorail
a good way to see Disneyland

ur, we walked back to the giant
he usual crowds that day, and
d our car. Driving out of the lot,
behind us and it turned on its
r vehicles around, it was pain-
g stopped. Why was a mystery,
e no stop signs or speed limit
g at a slow speed.

57

The police officer exited his patrol car and walked directly to my car door with a big ticket book in his hand. As I was handing the officer my drivers license, I thought this is the pits and why is this happening to us. Just then, Friederike did something brilliant that saved my day. She looked at me and at the officer and said, "This is terrible—here you are on your way to Vietnam and you are getting a ticket." The officer said, "My brother is in Vietnam now with the First Cavalry Division." He asked was I flying out from Oakland and I said yes, tomorrow. He closed his ticket book and said, "Now I am going to pull in front of you and you follow me out to the freeway." He put on his blue lights and gave us a police escort. As we were approaching the freeway, another police car was on the side of the road. An officer was standing outside his vehicle and saluted us as we drove by. I felt so humbled and so thankful that people really do care. To this day over forty years later, I still don't know why the officer stopped us. Maybe he was just bored and wanted to liven things up a bit. Friederike and I are glad it happened as it did. It showed again that some things are just going to happen and when they do we should worry less about the why and how and focus more on the good aspects. After all, the journey is the destination.

# The Wall Came Down

U nder the pressure of a movement for democratic change across Eastern Europe, the infamous Berlin Wall came down in 1989. Constructed in 1961 when Germany was divided between West Germany (Bundes Republic Deutschland) and East Germany (Deutsche Demokratik Republik). The wall separating Berlin and East Germany from the West was a stark symbol of tyranny and tragedy. The wall's collapse came with the reunification of Germany and ushered in an era of hope. During his visit to Berlin in 1963, President John F. Kennedy gave his "Ich bin ein Berliner" speech which the Germans loved and admired Kennedy. Later that year when Kennedy was assassinated in Dallas, Germany went into a prolonged state of mourning.

I was with the First US Infantry Division on a deployment from Fort Riley, Kansas to Wildflecken, Germany that tragic day in 1963. When it happened in Dallas, the time in Germany was seven hours later. That particular evening, I was having dinner at the home of a lovely German girl. After dinner, my girlfriend called a taxi to take me back to the Wildflecken Army post. Unaware of what had happened, when I got in the taxi the driver started talking in an excited tone about President Kennedy and others being shot. Several thoughts raced through my mind. Uppermost was could this be the beginning of another global conflict.

As the taxi entered the long street up the hill inside the post, all the lights were coming on. Especially noticeable were the lights at the ammunition bunkers and the sounds of the engines on our tanks that were being loaded with live ammunition. All this signaled a general alert status and not just another training exercise. When the taxi arrived in front of the Army BOQ (bachelor officers' quarters), my driver was already there in his full battle uniform sitting in our jeep waiting for me to rush inside and get dressed. He said to me, "Lieutenant don't worry we have a full tank of gas and I got the extra hand grenades we talked about." As a liaison team, our mission was to go to the various other military units in our sector to exchange overlays and battle formation plans with them.

Our Army unit went to its forward deployment area and sat there ready to engage any movement into West Germany by the opposing forces. There was no hostile action on the other side of the border because the Warsaw Pact forces were apparently unaware of the facts of the events in Dallas. Fortunately, no country had attacked the United States and World War III had not started that terrible day in Texas in 1963.

This was before the era of instant widespread coverage of news events and the prolific use of electronic devices.

My first visit to Berlin also occurred in 1963 and before President Kennedy's visit there.

I was stationed with the US Army in free West Germany. At that time, an element of the US Army Berlin Brigade gave tours into the city including the Soviet-held East Berlin. Another lieutenant from my unit and I took a tour into East Berlin. Our small tour bus made various stops. One was at the Soviet memorial. As we were walking toward a large statue, two Russian officers approached us. They were Soviet Army captains, so we as only lieutenants, saluted the Russians properly. They smiled and began talking to us in perfect English. Boris, the captain nearest me, looked at my parachutist wings and asked, "Did you go to jump school at Fort Benning, Georgia or to Fort Bragg, North Carolina?" I answered Fort Benning. Boris also complimented me on being a Ranger and added that Ranger school is a tough course. When asked what was my home state, I replied Tennessee. Right away, Boris knew the state capital was Nashville. Of course, nothing sensitive was discussed. The Russian captains were very sharp in their appearance and demeanor and it was obvious that they were not just average officers. My fellow lieutenant and I enjoyed the encounter, which was the high point of our visit into East Germany.

The second time I was in Berlin was 11 years later. The ugly wall was still there, but a lot of other things had changed. The most significant thing for me was my marriage to a beautiful Bavarian girl named Friederike. She was a citizen of West Germany before her naturalization later as American when we were living in the United States. To get to Berlin, which sat deep in communist East Germany, we took the train without stops. For Friederike, like other West Germans, she had only read about the terrible wall, but had never seen it. When she finally stood at the wall, the emotions of despair and gloom hit hard. The US Army officer and his wife, with whom we were staying in the American sector housing area, took us on a special tour of Berlin, including the infamous Checkpoint Charlie which was a major entry and exit point into East Berlin. At CP Charlie, we climbed up on the wooden stairs enabling us to see into the communist side. The utter bleakness of the area was formidable and depressing.

Directly to our front was a pill-box type cement guard post. A young East German soldier with a sub machine gun was looking at us through his binoculars, almost like it was a game. The soldier looked no older than 17 or 18 years old. He wore an ill-fitting field jacket and he looked sad. Unable to resist the urge, I flashed him a v-shaped peace symbol with my two fingers. It was clear that he saw the symbol. He climbed down the steps inside his guard post and appeared outside directly in front of the guard post which was out of sight of the Soviet-manned tower about 100 meters back inside the wall. The young soldier looked directly at me and flashed a peace symbol exactly as I did to him minutes earlier. This was an emotional moment for me and for other people nearby on freedom's side of the wall, including British, Canadians, French, West Germans and other Americans. No words were needed and tears came to my eyes and to the others who saw a piece of humanity that day. All of us had no doubt that the young soldier would rather be playing soccer, having a beer with his buddies or walking with his girl friend along the river than being a puppet in a sense-less guard post. Another emotional aspect of visiting the ugly wall were the numerous impromptu memorials of flowers and mementos marking spots where brave East Germans were shot trying to escape over the wall into the west and freedom.

# The Fourth Quarter

**D**id you ever look at an hourglass and watch the sand move through it? When you first turn it over to start the process, the sand at the top seems to move so slowly.

After several minutes, the rate of movement seems to stabilize or be consistent for a while.

In terms of human life, people often refer to this stage of around 50 years old as "middle aged." Thinking like an optimist, being 50 and middle aged, helps some people assume that they may make it to the century mark of 100. After the mid-point when we look again at the hourglass, the sand appears to start moving faster toward the bottom. For those of us already beyond the mid point, and entering life's final quarter, we wake up one day and reality tells us that we are already in the fourth quarter. The most frightening aspect of this stage is not necessarily the fact that we are getting old, but that we come to realize that we now have less time, or too little time, to complete our to-do lists or to finish the items on our "bucket list."

When we ask a small child how old they are, they often say, "three and a half or almost four" or something similar. If a senior citizen reveals their age verbally, they omit any fraction and simply say sixty-one or seventy, etc.

From this comparison, it can be assumed that youngsters look forward to moving up in age for the privileges it brings such as staying up later, playing on a sports team or taking drivers training. Conversely, seniors often prefer to slow down the aging process. A couple of phrases come to mind at this point. They are do not resent to grow old—many are denied the privilege. And a favorite of my older brother, Tony, was "Getting old is not for sissies." Certainly, life changes with age, but people still have some degree of control over the changes. Some braver, and generally more happy seniors, are able to tell themselves that "We don't quit playing because we get old, rather we get old because we quit playing." One of my wise Army buddies stated recently that, "When old men get together, they talk about aches, pains, medications, and politics. And when old women get together, they talk about old men." I can attest to the accuracy of the comment about old men, but I cannot verify the comment about old women because I don't know any old women. Maybe I have bent the arrow a little bit by denying to know any old women, but political correctness does have its place. At least that is what I have been told.

What happened to the youthful joy of playing marbles in the dirt, swinging on a vine in the woods, building a fort, catching lightening bugs (fireflies in some areas) and putting them in glass jars, tying sewing thread on the leg of a June bug and letting them fly tethered, picking blackberries for a pie or Mother to make jam, fishing in a creek with a cane pole, playing with a yoyo on a string, flying a homemade kite, camping out under the stars on a summer night, putting a penny on a railroad track to be flattened by the train, eating popcicles, and looking to the heavens on a star-filled night and saying "Star light, star bright the first star I saw tonight, I wish I may, I wish I might, have the wish I wish tonight." At bedtime, we still remember the prayer Mother taught us. It is "Now I lay me down to sleep, I pray the Lord my soul to keep. And if I should die before I wake, I pray the Lord my soul to take."

In the fourth quarter we also tend to be more honest with ourselves. By then, the mortgage is usually paid up, we are not writing resumes or looking for a new job, or worrying about how to move up the corporate ladder. Even after we retire officially, some of us are silly enough to get a part time job, or two like me, because retirement isn't always easy. It is comforting though to know that we are still working because we want to rather than because we have to. After retiring from a corporate job, I started teaching college courses part time and I enjoy it. In one of my chats with my friend Nick Chronis he asked me how I liked teaching. I said since I don't teach on Fridays, I get three-day weekends and that is nice. Nick paused for a moment and let me know that, as a guy who passed the course on retirement, he gets seven-day weekends. That is the way it is supposed to be. When I pass the course on retirement, I want to be like Nick.

Along with some of life's lessons revealed in the above chapters, my research into ethos and ethics discovered several excellent sources. One of my favorites and most helpful was "The Psychology of Winning" by Doctor Denis

Waitley. As the author-narrator, Doctor Waitley offers simple and profound principles shared by many great achievers. His outstanding program teaches us how to build self-esteem, motivation and self-discipline while developing the 10 qualities of a total winner. I recommend "The Psychology of Winning" to anyone seeking a deeper understanding of how to increase human effectiveness and how to live a better life.

# References

Jones, John, and Carlson, Daniel (2004). "Reputable Conduct—Ethical Issues in Policing and Corrections." Pearson Prentice Hall, New Jersey.

Josephson, Michael (n.d.). "The Bell, the Book, the Candle." The Josephson Institute for Ethics, California.

Ruiz, Don Miguel (1997). "The Four Agreements." Amber-Allen Publishing, Inc., California

Waitley, Denis (n.d.). "The Psychology of Winning." Nightingale-Conant Corporation, Chicago.

# About the Author

Herman Statum served as the Director of Corporate Security for a 42,000-member corporation with facilities nationwide including manufacturing plants, distribution centers and retail stores. He served as the Director of Security, Auditing and Training at the nation's largest farm and ranch retailer with 250 stores in 26 states. Herman also served as the Director of Information Security at the nation's largest healthcare corporation. As an airborne, ranger and special forces officer, Herman's career included 11 years overseas with two tours in Vietnam. He served as a Branch Chief at the Headquarters, Department of the Army Law Enforcement Division in the Pentagon and served as the Executive Director of the Department of Army Physical Review Board which was the Army Secretary's principal group managing protection of personnel, facilities, data systems and weapons of mass destruction world wide. Herman chaired the Washington, DC Chapter of the American Society for Industrial Security (ASIS) International and served six years on the ASIS Board of Directors. He holds a BS degree from Middle Tennessee State University and he has an MS degree, from the University of Southern California.

Herman is board certified as a CPP (Certified Protection Professional), certified as a CFE (Certified Fraud Examiner), certified in Homeland Security at the highest level (CHS-V), and is licensed as a PI (Private Investigator). He has taught at the elementary, high school and college levels and served on the curriculum advisory committees of four academic institutions. Herman is an instructor in criminal justice at Remington College and teaches courses on liability and ethics. He gives presentations on assets protection, loss prevention, crisis management, homeland security, and ethics to various associations and professional groups. Herman was born and raised in Shelbyville, Tennessee. He currently resides in Brentwood, Tennessee with his wife and daughter. He and his wife were recognized as generous donors by the Community Foundation of Middle Tennessee.

Herman was honored by the American Board for Certification in Homeland Security as the recipient of its Annual Leadership Award for his contributions to the homeland security program and to the security of the nation overall. In 2015, the Middle Tennessee Chapter of the American Society for Industrial Security (ASIS) International presented Herman with its new Lifetime Achievement Award for his distinguished career and his commitment to the advancement of the private security industry. The award bearing his name will be presented annually to a deserving ASIS member or a to a public safety official.